...If You Lived in WILLIAMSBURG in COLONIAL DAYS

BY BARBARA BRENNER

ILLUSTRATED BY JENNY WILLIAMS

Colonial Williamsburg Foundation

Williamsburg, Virginia

SCHOLASTIC INC.

New York Toronto London Auckland Sydney
Mexico City New Delhi Hong Kong

CONTENTS

◆ ◆ ◆

Introduction 4

What did Williamsburg look like in 1770? 6

How many people lived in Williamsburg?......................8

What was Market Square? 9

Who shopped in Market Square? 10

How did people pay for what they bought?.................12

Where did people go after shopping? 14

What was a colonial tavern like? 14

What kind of clothes did men and boys wear?............16

What kind of clothes did women and girls wear? 18

Where did people get their clothes? 22

What did poor people wear?......................................23

Were there barbers and hairdressers in colonial Williamsburg?..........24

What did Williamsburg houses look like? 26

How were Williamsburg houses furnished?.................29

What were the bedrooms like? 31

Where was the bathroom? 33

Where were the kitchen and dining room? 35

Who did the cooking? 37

What did people in Williamsburg eat? 38

What did people drink? 39

Was there such a thing as party food?.......................40

How was food kept from spoiling? 42

Did everyone have a garden? 43

What did they grow on the big plantations? 44

Did people know that using tobacco was unhealthy? 45

Were there schools in Williamsburg? 46

Did girls and boys learn the same things? 48

Did children have storybooks to read? 49

Did enslaved black people have a chance for education? 50

Were there many churches in colonial Williamsburg? 51

What did children do for fun? 52

Did people keep animals as pets? 54

Did families spend time together? 55

Did enslaved people have any chance for fun? 58

What work could a boy do when he grew up? 59

What was an apprentice? 61

What kinds of jobs were open to women? .62

Were there paying jobs for African-Americans? 64

What happened when you got sick or were hurt? 65

Did doctors know about "shots"? 66

How were children expected to behave? 68

What happened when a child misbehaved? 69

What happened to people who broke the law? 70

What happened to slaves who broke the laws? 72

Who made the laws for colonial Williamsburg? 73

Why was there an English governor? 74

Why were the colonists angry at the British? 75

Williamsburg today 78

Introduction

It's hard to imagine a time when there was no United States. But before 1776, America consisted of only thirteen colonies. All of them were in the eastern part of the country. All of them were ruled by England.

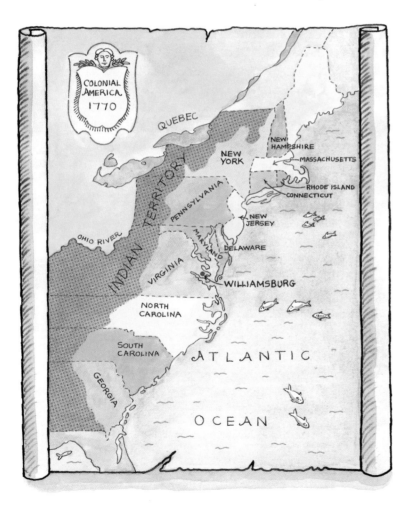

The colony of Virginia became the most prosperous of the thirteen, thanks to its mild southern weather, its rich soil, and its profitable crop — tobacco.

One of Virginia's most bustling towns was Williamsburg — named for King William III of England. It started out as a tiny frontier outpost called Middle Plantation. By the early 1700s, it had become the capital of Virginia and was renamed Williamsburg. Known as the showplace of the colonies, its list of prominent citizens and visitors read like a "Who's Who" of important colonial leaders.

Suppose you had lived in colonial Williamsburg in 1770, six years before America declared independence from England. What would it have been like?

Let's take a look.

Nursery rhymes were probably the very first poems you heard when you were very young. You would have learned some of those same rhymes if you lived back in 1770. As you read this book, you'll see some of them again. Notice how much they tell about what life was like in those days.

What did Williamsburg look like in 1770?

At a time when most people lived on farms, Williamsburg was a thriving town. It had wide streets, large public buildings, and elegant shops. It had a theater.

The handsome H-shaped Capitol building with the British flag flying above it was at one end of town. At the other end was the college — William and Mary, the second college in America.

On the main streets, houses stood side by side with shops that sold all kinds of goods and services. Many of the houses had gardens.

In and outside of Williamsburg, there were small- and medium-sized farms. Farther away from town were large plantations — hundreds of acres of land planted in tobacco, corn, and wheat.

How many people lived in Williamsburg?

About two thousand. Half were white settlers or the descendants of white people who had originally come from England, Scotland, or Ireland.

A few of them were wealthy, educated planters or merchants — the *gentry*. A larger number were middle-class farmers, storekeepers, tradesmen, and their families — the *middling sort*. The rest were poor folk who worked as servants, laborers, or field hands.

The other half of Williamsburg's population were African-Americans. Most of them were slaves. Unlike the white people, they hadn't come to America because they wanted to. They had been captured and brought from Africa to work in Virginia. For the slave owners, it was a good arrangement — steady help in the fields and houses, with no wages to pay. For the enslaved people, it was totally different. Although they were given food, clothing, and a place to sleep, they were treated like property instead of human beings.

What was Market Square?

It was a large, open area in the middle of town. Several days a week, farmers, tradesmen, and slaves came there to sell their wares. You would have seen carts loaded with eggs, meat, milk, and butter; with crabs and oysters; with vegetables and fruit. Sometimes people brought cows, sheep, pigs, and chickens to sell. In fact, on certain days there were almost as many animals on the street as people!

Everyone knew that to get the best items from the market you had to come early. The market opened at dawn. By noon, the fattest pigs, the freshest fish, and the juiciest fruits were already sold.

To market, to market
To buy a fat pig.
Home again, home again,
Jiggety jig.

Who shopped in Market Square?

Housewives came to buy groceries. Slaves came to shop for their masters. Sometimes, a few Pamunkey Indians would show up with pottery to sell.

There were always plenty of children of all ages. Baby carriages hadn't been invented yet, so mothers could be seen balancing babies in their arms as they poked the fruits and vegetables for ripeness. When you went to market, you might have helped your mother shop or looked after your younger brother or sister.

Occasionally black people were brought to Market Square for a terrible reason — to be sold at auction as if they were horses or cows. Imagine how you would have felt, seeing your father or mother bought by a stranger. You would have known that you were likely to be separated from your family, perhaps forever.

How did people pay for what they bought?

In colonial Virginia, you could pay for goods with coins. The coins had been made in other countries and were brought to Williamsburg by merchants and traders. The most common coins were Spanish silver.

The *value* of the money was based on the English system. Merchants weighed foreign coins to figure out their value in *pence* (d), *shillings* (s), and *pounds* (£). To make change, they would cut up a coin.

A pound in any form was a great deal of money. It was several weeks' pay for many people. If you were lucky, your parents might give you a few pence to spend at the market. You could buy a pencil for 3.25 pence or a pack of playing cards for 7.5 pence. But a pound of chocolate would have been beyond your budget at two shillings and sixpence (2/6).

I had sixpence,
jolly jolly sixpence.
I had sixpence
To last me all my life.

I had twopence to spend,
and twopence to lend,
and twopence to take home
To my wife.

The most common way grown-ups made a big purchase, such as a horse, was by using a tobacco certificate. A tobacco certificate was something like a check. But instead of being backed by a certain amount of money in the bank, it was backed by a certain amount of tobacco in a warehouse. You could buy a horse, a wagon, or a whole set of furniture with a tobacco certificate.

You could also trade, or barter, instead of using money. If you were selling corn and you wanted to buy a rooster, for example, you might give so many bushels of corn for the rooster.

Where did people go after shopping?

Some people went straight home. Others stayed to talk with friends, or to watch a street performer. Still others went down the street to a tavern to get something to eat and drink.

You might have gone with your family to Chowning's Tavern on a market day.

Chowning's (say CHEWnings) was right near Market Square. It was one of at least five taverns in Williamsburg. Several of them were run by women.

What was a colonial tavern like?

It was a kind of combination restaurant and hotel. People went there for a meal or a drink or to stay overnight. The worst part of staying overnight was that you usually had to share a room and sometimes even a bed with a stranger.

When you stepped out of Chowning's Tavern, you were on Duke of Gloucester Street, the main street of Williamsburg. It was unusually wide for a colonial street — one hundred feet — and it was nearly a mile long. But it was made of sand, so it could be mighty dusty walking there on a dry summer day. And in rainy weather, the water collected in the ruts and the sand turned to mud. Your shoes got coated, and your clothing got splashed when a carriage or a wagon went by.

What kind of clothes did men and boys wear?

Baby boys and girls of colonial Williamsburg were dressed almost alike, in a long gown (dress), a *shift* (a nightgownlike garment), or a shirt. Early on, parents began to train their children to stand up straight. As a toddler, you would have been put into stays, a kind of cloth brace stiffened with whalebone, which would keep your back straight and give you good posture.

When a boy was about four years old, he was *breeched.* He graduated from babyhood to boyhood by getting his first pair of *breeches,* pants that came down just over the knees, the way men's breeches did. The stays came off, and the boy dressed like a smaller version of his father.

Gentry men and boys wore breeches of silk, satin, or fine linen. If you were of the middling sort or poor, your breeches were likely to be wool,

cotton, or coarse linen. Most men and boys didn't wear underpants. Instead, they tucked the long tails of their shirts inside their breeches.

Next came a *waistcoat* (vest), a coat, and maybe a three-cornered hat. The cut of the coat helped your posture by pulling your shoulders back.

Neckties didn't look like they do today. Some men wore *cravats*, which were long, narrow cloths that wrapped around the shirt collars. Other men wore bands of white linen called *stocks*.

Stockings and shoes finished off the outfit.

There wasn't much variety in men's and boys' clothes. About all you could do to make a more original fashion statement was to wear a different color or add interesting trim.

Diddle diddle dumpling, my son John
Went to bed with his breeches on,
One stocking off, and one stocking on;
Diddle diddle dumpling, my son John.

What kind of clothes did women and girls wear?

Girls and women wore a lot more clothing than they do today. Getting dressed in the morning was quite a production. It started with your shift. (You wouldn't have worn underpants.) It's likely you already had on your shift because you had worn it to bed. Next you would change from your nightcap to the one you wore during the day. Women and girls wore caps almost all the time.

Then you might pull on your long stockings. They were held up by ribbon garters tied around the leg.

Next came the *stays* to help you stand up straight. Well-to-do women might add *hoops* to make their skirts stand out.

Then you added your *petticoat* or petticoats. After that came your *pocket*, a separate pouch you tied around your waist.

Next you put on an *outer petticoat* and a *short gown*, a *frock*, or a *gown*. An outer petticoat was like a skirt, and the short gown you wore with it was like a jacket. Many middling-sort and poorer women and girls wore this kind of outfit, especially when they were working.

A frock was a dress that some gentry and middling-sort girls wore, usually with a colored sash. A gown was a dress that well-to-do women wore. The skirts of an outer petticoat, frock, or gown came down to the ankles.

Lucy Locket lost her pocket,
Kitty Fisher found it;
Nothing in it, nothing in it
But the binding round it.

Little Polly Flinders
Sat among the cinders
Warming her pretty little toes;
Her mother came and caught her,
Whipped her little daughter
For spoiling her nice new clothes.

When you were working, you usually wore an apron to protect your clothes. When you went out, you might put a kerchief around your neck to shield your skin from the sun or to keep warm — and for decoration. You also put a hat on top of your cap when you left the house.

When you went to bed, you took off everything but your shift, put on your nightcap — and probably heaved a sigh of relief to get rid of all that clothing!

Women accented their clothes with kerchiefs, ribbons, and other items copied from European styles. A girl might shop for these trimmings at Margaret Hunter's shop or John Greenhow's store. Both were on Duke of Gloucester Street.

Where did people get their clothes?

There were a few homes in Williamsburg where the women still made all the clothes for the children. Your mother might have made your frocks and breeches — and then remade them for your younger brothers and sisters when you grew out of them.

Some wealthy families had their clothes made to order and shipped from England.

The town also had shops where you could buy items of clothing, including leather shoes. Fancy fabric shoes were called *stuff*. They had to be imported from England.

What did poor people wear?

Poor and enslaved people's style of dress had to fit their labor. Women wore cool shifts and loose-fitting skirts called *petticoats*. They wore kerchiefs or head wraps on their heads when they worked in the fields in summer.

Men wore trousers, makeshift shirts, and broad-brimmed hats. Sometimes slaves recycled old clothes that their masters had discarded and made them over for themselves or their children.

Were there barbers and hairdressers in colonial Williamsburg?

You probably would have had your hair cut at home. People also went to barbershops. Charlton House was one Williamsburg barbershop that was in operation around 1770. Edward Charlton advertised that he could give a man a shave and a haircut or "dress" a lady's hair and sell her fake curls to add to her hairdo.

He could make a wig for a lady or a gentleman. If you were a gentleman's son, he might have made you your first wig, or *peruke*, when you were as young as eight or nine. Some rich girls wore wigs by the time they were teenagers.

Barber, barber, shave a pig,
How many hairs will make a wig?
"Four and twenty, that's enough."
Give the poor barber a pinch of snuff.

Wigs could be made of horsehair or goat hair. The best ones, however, were made from human hair. Poor girls sold their hair to wigmakers so that gentry men and women could wear wigs. The people who bought the wigs would usually shave off their own hair so the wig would fit better!

Wigs of white hair were considered the most stylish. They were also the most expensive. If you couldn't afford a white wig, you powdered yours to make it look white.

Poor people didn't wear wigs. They were too expensive.

What did Williamsburg houses look like?

There were a few roughly made wooden houses on the backstreets. Some of them had oiled paper in the windows instead of glass. The more up-to-date homes had glass windows and were built of brick or painted wood. They often had an upstairs and a downstairs.

No houses had electric lights. You would have used candles. Heat for warmth and cooking came mainly from open fireplaces.

Everyone worried about fire. There would have been a bucket handy to the well, for putting out a fire in your own house or a neighbor's. It was no wonder people who could afford it built houses of brick.

Many middling-sort families in Williamsburg were farmers. If you came from a farm family, your house would most likely have been at the end of town, where there was a little more grass for your sheep and cows — and less dust.

If your father was a miller, you would have had a windmill on your property to grind the corn and wheat before it was sold.

The gentry lived in elegant mansions in and around Williamsburg. Some of their homes had as many as eight rooms and several outbuildings. Sometimes the rooms had plaster walls instead of wooden ones. Sometimes they were painted or papered with fancy imported wallpaper.

If your father was a tradesman or merchant, you would have lived close to the main part of town. The house was often attached to a shop or an office.

There was an old woman
Lived under a hill,
And if she's not gone
She lives there still.

Enslaved people who worked in town slept close to the master they worked for. Some slept in out-buildings, such as the kitchen or laundry, or in the main house on a mat outside their master's or mistress's room. Those on farms also lived in outbuildings or spaces in the house.

Slaves on plantations often lived in one-room huts in a separate area called a *quarter*. Sometimes the slaves built a fence around their houses like the ones they remembered from their African villages.

How were Williamsburg houses furnished?

Most likely you would have had chairs, tables, beds, chests, and cupboards in your house. If you were of the middling sort, your furniture would have been made by a local tradesman or by your father.

If you were gentry, your home would have had much more furniture. Many of the rooms would have looked like those in British houses, with imported hand-carved furniture, silver candlesticks, chandeliers, carpets, and wall hangings.

A large house in town or on a plantation may have had a harpsichord or a spinet that the girls of the house were taught to play. (Girls also learned the English guitar.) Boys learned the flute or the violin. There was talk of a marvelous new instrument called the pianoforte, or piano, but very few people in the colonies owned one.

In some homes, dishes on the cupboard and framed prints were the only decorations. Photography hadn't been

invented yet, so there were no family photographs. Some well-to-do residents had their portraits painted by artists who had traveled to the area.

People didn't hang pictures in their bedrooms. They hung them in more "public" spaces such as the dining room, parlor, and main entrance hall, which they called the *passage*.

What were the bedrooms like?

Many houses had at least one separate room for sleeping. Mother, father, and the baby usually slept there. Another room in the house often doubled as a bedroom for the older children at night. In some houses, children slept in a loft — a large, open space above the stairs.

What we call mattresses today were beds back then. Some beds were stuffed with horsehair or feathers and put on a wooden frame called a *bedstead*.

Bedsteads looked something like our beds of today, but weren't nearly as comfortable. There were no springs under the bed, just ropes. You and your sisters and brothers might have slept together in one big bedstead. It was cozy in winter but not cool in the summer!

There were no screens on any of the windows. You would have pulled netting over your bed to keep out the flies and mosquitoes.

There were no twin beds, but if space was limited, you might have had a *trundle* bed. It was rolled — *trundled* — under your parents' bedstead during the day.

Well-to-do folks had soft feather beds with canopies above them and curtains that closed around the bed to keep out drafts.

Some people slept on the floor on beds stuffed with straw—a sort of colonial sleeping bag.

Where was the bathroom?

There were no bathrooms.

What? Isn't a bathroom necessary? Absolutely. That's why there was a small hut behind each Williamsburg home. It was called the *necessary*. There was also a chamber pot under the bed for emergencies and cold nights.

In 1770, even the most elegant house in Williamsburg was without hot or cold running water. Someone had to bring water inside or you had to go out to the well when you wanted to wash your hands.

Some people did brush their teeth in colonial times. They either used a toothbrush they bought at the store or a piece of chewed licorice root. Flossing was unheard of. That may have been one

reason why apothecaries cleaned and pulled teeth and did other dental work.

Keeping clean was a hard job. Bathing meant carrying in water from the well, heating the water, then scrubbing up and wiping off before the water got cold. So if you lived in colonial Williamsburg, you wouldn't have taken a bath very often. Between times, some people doused themselves with lavender water.

Where were the kitchen and dining room?

If you lived in a large house, your kitchen was in a separate building. It sat apart from the main house so that you could get away from the smell and the heat of cooking during the hot Virginia summers. Not many houses in Williamsburg had this feature. Most people did their cooking in the fireplace in what was often the main room of the house. You might have eaten all your meals there.

A large house had a separate room for dining. In many houses, it doubled as a kind of "family room." Tables and chairs were brought out into the middle of the room for meals.

After meals, the dining furniture was pushed back up against a wall so the room could be used for other purposes. It was called "putting the room in repose." It might have been one of your chores.

Who did the cooking?

The girls and women of the house prepared the meals. If you were of the middling sort, your parents might have had a slave girl.

If you were gentry, you were likely to have several enslaved people working in your kitchen. Your mother supervised them and taught them how to cook. They might have taught your mother some recipes that came from their African homeland. Today's "southern cooking" comes from a blend of these two traditions.

What did people in Williamsburg eat?

They ate many of the same things we eat today — baked ham, potted or stewed beef, roast turkey, fried chicken, and fish.

There were apple and peach trees all over the Williamsburg area, and the colonists ate these and other fruits.

Common garden vegetables included peas, beans, turnips, lettuce, onions, carrots, sweet and white potatoes, and squash. Corn, which the original settlers had learned about from the Native Americans, was cooked dozens of ways. Besides being made into bread, it was roasted on the ear, fried, baked, boiled, and eaten as a cereal. Hominy, corn pudding, corn bread, and hoecakes (so named because the early settlers sometimes put them in the oven on the blade of a hoe) were just a few of the dishes made from corn. Because it was so cheap and plentiful, corn was a common food of poor folk.

Pease porridge hot,
Pease porridge cold,
Pease porridge in the pot
Nine days old.

Most people worked for an hour or two before they ate breakfast. Dinner — the big meal of the day — was served about two o'clock. For supper, often you would have leftovers from dinner.

What did people drink?

Tea was extraordinarily popular. It wasn't only the taste. Tea was special because it came all the way from China. As soon as company arrived, out came the teapot and the tea set — imported from England if you were of the middling sort or gentry.

But tea wasn't the only drink available. Children as well as grown-ups drank milk, coffee, wine, apple cider, home-made beer, and — occasionally — "spirits" made from local fruits such as persimmons and peaches.

Molly, my sister, and I fell out,
And what do you think it was all about?
She loved coffee and I loved tea,
And that was the reason we couldn't agree.

Was there such a thing as party food?

Ordinarily folks made special foods for holidays and birthdays. They had picnics and covered-dish suppers where everyone brought something. The "something" might be anything from a freshly caught fish to a rabbit stew, a ham, or a fresh fruit pie.

Plantation owners and other gentry went all out for a party. A wedding or other celebration often lasted for several days. During that time, there was a constant stream of food and drink laid out on big banquet tables. Breakfast,

dinner, and supper for guests were all huge meals. Wealthy people felt that if they served only one main course they would look "hard up" — that is, poor. So there were often five or six different kinds of meats, fish, and fowl, and lots of wine, beer, cider, rum, and brandy for the grown-ups.

You also had a choice of several desserts — pies, cakes, candy, and perhaps a *trifle*, a rich cake made of jelly roll, custard, cream, rum, and wine. (Although it was called a *trifle*, it was anything but!)

If your parents gave a big party or *ball*, you and the other children would have eaten in another room and been waited on by servants.

How was food kept from spoiling?

That was a big problem. Refrigerators hadn't been invented yet. Some foods had to be eaten right away. Others were prepared in various ways to give them a longer shelf life. If you lived in colonial times, you would have eaten food pickled, potted, sugared, salted, smoked, and dried — all ways of preparing food that kept it from spoiling.

As they were figuring out ways to keep, or preserve, foods, southern colonists created such tasty dishes as Virginia cured ham and many other recipes that we enjoy today. In fact, the word *preserves* — the name for certain jams — is a reminder of why the food was prepared that way.

Did everyone have a garden?

Many townspeople bought fruits and vegetables at the markets. But other people had a "kitchen garden." If your mother kept a kitchen garden, she might have grown vegetables for eating, herbs for seasoning, and plants to use as medicine. A favorite vegetable was peas. "New peas" were started as soon as the soil could be worked in the spring.

If your family had a kitchen garden, one of your chores from a very early age would have been to lend a hand planting, weeding, and watering. You also would have been the official bug-squasher and rabbit-chaser. Gardening was an important chore. Some families started their little gardeners off when they were as young as five.

Not everything was grown for eating. In the spring and summer, you would have smelled the scent of English roses and other fragrant flowers growing in Williamsburg yards.

Mary, Mary,　　　　　　*With silver bells,*
Quite contrary,　　　　　*and cockle shells,*
How does your garden grow?　*And pretty maids all in a row.*

What did they grow on the big plantations?

Tobacco was the crop that had made Virginia planters so prosperous. You would have known all about tobacco. You would have seen field hands picking and curing it. You would have watched it being loaded onto ships that took it to foreign countries.

You might have seen your father and his friends smoking leaf tobacco in pipes. And sometimes instead of smoking, they might have taken a pinch of ground-up tobacco leaf, called *snuff*, and inhaled it through their noses.

Did people know that using tobacco was unhealthy?

Some people did. In 1604, King James I of England had said that tobacco was "a custom lothsome to the eye, hateful to the nose, harmeful to the braine, dangerous to the lungs. . . ." In spite of the king's wise statement, there was a regular craze for tobacco, especially in Europe. From the time John Rolfe (Pocahontas's husband) sent the first crop of sweet tobacco from Virginia to England in 1614, millions of pounds of tobacco were sent across the seas.

By the 1750s, the soil in Virginia had begun to show the bad effects of growing only one crop year after year. If your father was a farmer or planter, he probably had begun to grow wheat and corn on part of his land.

Whatever was grown, the enslaved African-Americans did most of the heavy work. The slaves planted, weeded, and picked. Even women and children as young as seven or eight worked long hours in the fields.

Were there schools in Williamsburg?

There were no free public schools in all of Virginia. Some parents taught their children to read and write at home. The Bible often served as reader, workbook, and storybook all in one.

But what if your parents didn't know how to read? Some grown-ups in Williamsburg couldn't read or write; they signed legal papers with an X instead of their names. Still, many wanted their children to be educated. For a small fee, a schoolmaster or schoolmistress could be hired to teach a group of children of various ages how to read and *cipher* (do arithmetic). In town, these classes were often held in the house where the teacher lived. Outside town, lessons might be held in a structure in an abandoned tobacco field, so they came to be called *old field schools*.

A dillar, a dollar,
A ten o'clock scholar,
What makes you come so soon.
You used to come at ten o'clock,
And now you come at noon.

If you were gentry, school came to you. Children of the rich had private tutors who lived with them. Sometimes there was a separate wing or even a separate building set aside for a schoolroom. Sisters and brothers of various ages went there together. The hours were long — from early morning to six o'clock, with a recess for breakfast and another one an hour or two long before dinner.

Did girls and boys learn the same things?

Boys and girls were taught to read, write, and cipher. But a girl's education usually stopped after that. Gentry boys continued their schooling with a tutor and took such subjects as Latin and Greek, Hebrew, history, and geography. Then they went on to college, either the College of William and Mary in Williamsburg or a university in Europe. Boys could become lawyers, doctors, clergymen, or other professionals.

For girls, it was a different story. Girls couldn't study Latin and Greek, medicine, or law no matter how rich or smart they were. Priscilla Carter, who came from one of Williamsburg's wealthiest families, didn't learn multiplication and division until she was about fifteen years old.

Did children have storybooks to read?

There were no lending libraries in Williamsburg in 1770. Your parents could order books from England or buy them at the Printing Office on Duke of Gloucester Street. A Bible was the only book some families owned, although others had books for both children and adults.

In addition to nursery rhymes, you might have read classic English children's stories such as *Jack the Giant Killer*. As you got older, you would have graduated to popular novels — *Gulliver's Travels* and *The Adventures of Robinson Crusoe*.

A few Williamsburg homes had libraries. Both George Wythe and Peyton Randolph, two of the town's most respected men, had libraries. William Byrd, the owner of a Virginia plantation, had a library of several thousand books. However, his wife, being a woman, wasn't allowed to borrow them. Fortunately, not all men in colonial Virginia felt this way. Some fathers bought books for their daughters, and many gentry women were well read.

Did enslaved black people have a chance for education?

Some masters and mistresses taught their slaves to read and write. Masters sometimes saw to it that their male slaves learned a trade. Some enslaved girls were taught household skills such as cooking, doing laundry, cleaning, and spinning.

For fourteen years, about thirty African-American children per year attended the Bray School, a charity school run by the Anglican Church. Here enslaved boys and girls were taught to read and write, to learn "the true spelling of words," and to understand the Christian religion.

Girls learned manners and "knitting, sewing, and such other things as may be useful to their owners." Boys, besides learning manners, were taught arithmetic so that they could keep accounts for their masters.

Slave children went to school part-time for three years or until their owners put them to work at home.

Were there many churches in colonial Williamsburg?

Every Sunday morning, church bells rang out from Bruton Parish Church on Duke of Gloucester Street. The brick Anglican church, built early in the 1700s, was the one and only official church in Williamsburg. Free residents of Williamsburg were required to attend at least once a month. If they didn't, they had to pay a fine.

If you were an enslaved person you could come to services only if you had gotten permission from your master. You had to sit in a different section of the church. College students, too, sat in a separate area.

What we call Sunday school usually took place at home. Families spent at least part of Sunday reading the Bible and helping their children learn certain passages by heart. You weren't allowed to play games or to read anything but the Bible on Sunday.

Here is the church
And here is the steeple.
Open the door
And here's all the people.
(An old finger play)

What did children do for fun?

Life wasn't all chores and lessons. For most children, there was time for play. In the side streets and backyards of Williamsburg, there was plenty of room for rolling a hoop or flying a kite. There were no cars, of course. But in the street, you did have to keep an eye out for horses and wagons.

Children played jump rope and hopscotch and tag and hide-and-seek. Boys chased girls and teased them. *Checks*, a game that was played with peach pits, was very popular with the girls. Boys played ball games such as *cricket*; *fives*, a kind of handball; and *base-ball*, which wasn't much like today's game. It was played in a field marked off to form a triangle.

Georgie Porgie, puddin' and pie,
Kissed the girls and made them cry.
When the boys came out to play,
Georgie Porgie ran away.

Indoors, young girls played "house." They made believe they were cooking or cleaning or spinning. Gentry and middling-sort girls had miniature tea sets and held tea parties to which their dolls were invited.

Girls called their dolls *babies* even though most of the dolls were dressed in grown-up clothes. Some children had hand-carved dolls made by their father or a local wood-carver. Other girls owned a store-bought doll.

Older boys and girls played with cards and board games and worked on puzzles. Many puzzles taught something. For example, one geography puzzle was a map of the thirteen colonies.

Did people keep animals as pets?

Families kept dogs and cats, but they were usually more than just pets. They were workers that earned their keep. Dogs were used for hunting, herding sheep, and keeping wild animals away from the livestock. Cats took care of the mouse population in houses and barns. Pet turtles ate bugs in the house.

You might have had a pet squirrel and carried it around in your pocket or kept it in a little cage. Mockingbirds, too, were highly prized as pets.

A horse was a work animal. But for the gentry, riding horseback was a sport and a sign of being "somebody." An upperclass boy looked forward to having his own horse.

Did families spend time together?

In some ways, family life in 1770 was not too different from the way it is today. Most parents tried to spend time with their children. If they could, they went places and did things together.

Going to the fair in April and December was a popular family outing. At the fair, there were footraces to run, soaped pigs to catch, raffle prizes to win. As night fell, there were fireworks to watch.

Families spent time at home playing musical instruments or singing. Other times they played games such as blindman's buff and charades, as well as board and card games.

Virginians of all ages loved to dance. Ordinary folks learned the steps on their own. For the well-to-do, there

were dancing teachers who taught the minuet and country dances. It was extremely important for gentry children to dance well. The more steps you knew, the more popular you were at balls and assemblies. In some circles, a girl's popularity was judged by how quickly she wore out her dancing shoes!

Puppet shows were popular with everyone. One show called *Babes in the Wood* played in Williamsburg. It featured wooden puppets four feet high that, according to one observer, "appeared to be alive." If you had been there on one of the days this show was playing, you might have seen a future president — Thomas Jefferson — in the audience.

The theater on Waller Street in back of the Capitol building had something for everyone. Grown-ups went there to see a play by William Shakespeare or the latest popular comedy.

Did enslaved people have any chance for fun?

Black and white children played the same games together when they were young. Then, at about age five, they were separated. After that, the African-American children spent what little free time they had with other children of color. In spite of their long work hours, black families and friends sometimes managed to get together at night and on Sundays to sing, dance, and exchange stories.

Often, instead of joining such a get-together, one of the slaves would disappear into the woods on a *nightwalk*. A nightwalk was a visit, usually in secret, to a husband, wife, or child on a neighboring plantation. An enslaved person would often travel half the night and risk a beating for the chance to spend a little time with a loved one.

What work could a boy do when he grew up?

A boy often grew up to do what his father did. If he was the son of a farmer, he was likely to go into farming. If his father was a planter, he might become a planter, and maybe a lawyer, too. The son of a merchant might go into business. But many boys, especially those of the middling sort, needed to learn a trade. They started thinking about their future when they were about ten years old.

One choice was to become a blacksmith. James Anderson had a shop on Francis Street. He made all kinds of metal tools and could repair a musket as good as new. In the mid-1770s, when the Revolutionary War came, Mr. Anderson made and repaired weapons. A boy working for James Anderson would have helped supply the American troops with guns.

A boy might decide to model himself after Benjamin Powell. Mr. Powell was a successful *undertaker*, which in the 1700s was a building contractor, not a funeral director. Benjamin Powell built the tower and steeple on Bruton Parish Church. He had a fine house on Waller Street with a separate office building next door.

Being a cabinetmaker was another useful and highly skilled trade. Benjamin Bucktrout, who lived at the north end of town, made furniture. He also repaired harpsichords and spinets and made coffins.

Elkanah Deane, who lived on Prince George Street, had a busy coach-making shop. He and his workers built many of the carts, wagons, and carriages you would have seen on the streets of Williamsburg.

After a boy and his family decided what trade was best for him, his parents arranged for him to become an apprentice.

Seesaw, Margery Daw,
Jack shall have a new master.
He shall have but a penny a day,
Because he won't work any faster.

What was an apprentice?

Being an apprentice was a kind of work-study program. In colonial times, a boy was sent to work without pay for a tradesman — a carpenter or printer, for example. In return, the man taught the boy his trade.

The apprentice lived with his master for as long as seven years. At the end of that time, he was considered a *journeyman*. He could now get a paying job with another master or go into partnership with the man who had trained him.

What kinds of jobs were open to women?

In colonial America, most girls got married and became housewives. If you lived in Williamsburg in the 1700s, you probably would have gotten married at around age twenty.

A great many household tasks had to be done by hand, and a girl learned how to do them at a young age. Usually her mother taught her, but if she came from a poor family or if her mother had died, she might be "bound out" to another family for instruction.

By the time she was eight or nine, a girl knew enough about sewing to make a cap and a shirt. A middling-sort or gentry girl often took lessons to learn how to make a *sampler*, which was a stitched cloth piece designed to show her needlework skills. Later she also learned how to cook, spin, make candles and soap, and do many other things.

My maid Mary, she minds the dairy,
While I go a-hoeing and mowing each morn;
Gaily run the reel and the little spinning wheel,
While I am singing and mowing my corn.

In colonial times — like today — married women often had two jobs. Besides taking care of the house, a woman might have a small butter-and-eggs business, or she might spin cloth for customers, or sell surplus vegetables from the kitchen garden. Sometimes women helped their husbands run a store or tavern.

There were female farmers who plowed and sowed and harvested the crops side by side with their husbands.

There were also some female storekeepers and barbers in Williamsburg and one printer, Clementina Rind. Often these tradeswomen learned their husbands' businesses after they married.

Women also were teachers. And some women worked as midwives. Midwives helped women have their babies and care for their children when they were sick. In the colonies, women had their babies at home. A midwife instead of a doctor usually helped with the delivery.

There was a little woman,
As I have heard tell,
She went to market
Her eggs for to sell. . . .

Were there paying jobs for African-Americans?

Most African-Americans in Williamsburg were enslaved. They had no power over their futures. However, there were a few free blacks in Williamsburg. John Rawlinson was one of them. He was a *cordwainer*, or shoemaker. Rawlinson had a good business and property. He himself owned a slave.

Other free blacks were *carters* (people who hauled goods), farmers, laundresses, or *coopers* (people who make or repair wooden casks).

What happened when you got sick or were hurt?

Your mother, your big sister, or some other woman of the house took care of you. You were likely to get a home remedy. Here are a few that might have been tried on you:

To stop bleeding, apply a cobweb.

A toothache will disappear if three deep cuts are made in the northern side of a tree at sundown and blood from the tooth is transferred to the tree.

If you have a wart, rub it with a radish.

Jack and Jill went up the hill
To fetch a pail of water.
Jack fell down and broke his crown,
And Jill came tumbling after.

So up Jack got and home did trot,
As fast as he could caper,
To old Dame Dob, who patched his nob
With vinegar and brown paper.

If you didn't get better with such treatments, it was time to send for the doctor. For some ailments, you might be given a *vomit* or a *purge*. For another illness, you could have had a plaster put on your chest. The doctor might try to get your fever down by bleeding you. If you had a swelling, he might put a live leech on the wound to suck out the blood. All these measures were supposed to help your body heal.

There were several *apothecaries* in Williamsburg. An apothecary was a druggist-doctor. He made, imported, and sold medicines, in addition to treating sick patients.

Did doctors know about "shots"?

It was possible to get inoculated against smallpox. Other than that, vaccinations that protect against disease were almost unknown in the colonies. People of all ages died of diseases that today we don't even think about.

Parents tried to send their children to stay with relatives when an epidemic struck Williamsburg. In spite of these precautions, there was hardly a family that hadn't lost at least one child to such illnesses as scarlet fever, smallpox, and whooping cough. The little cemetery behind Bruton Parish Church had many graves of young children.

How were children expected to behave?

You were expected to obey the "dos" and "don'ts" laid down by your parents and society:

Don't be saucy (sassy) to your mother.
Don't wear your clothes until you can see the dirt.
Don't lie with your dog.
Before you speak, make a bow or a curtsy. . . .
Be courteous to the servants, because they are your inferiors; but for the same reason, never be familiar with them.

And last but certainly not least . . .

Whatever your parents order you to do is right, therefore do it with a good will and readiness.

Come when you're called,
Do what you're bid,
Shut the door after you,
And never be chid.

But like children of every century, the children of colonial Virginia sometimes misbehaved. Girls argued and got into scratching and hair-pulling fights. Boys snatched off someone's wig or broke a window playing ball or played in the brickyard and hurled *brickbats* — the small leftover pieces of brick — at one another. (Today to "hurl a brickbat" means to insult someone.)

What happened when a child misbehaved?

A great many parents of the eighteenth century still believed in paddling, spanking, and whipping with a cane. Some of them took care of that chore themselves. A boy in colonial Williamsburg might be whipped by his father for a number of reasons — even for not having his shoes shined.

Other parents left discipline up to the teacher or tutor. One dancing teacher boasted that he hit his female students if they didn't do the steps correctly.

What happened to people who broke the law?

People accused of crimes were put in jail in the county where they lived. They stayed there, bound in leg irons or shackles, until county justices of the peace looked into their case. These local justices made the decisions in all minor crimes as well as in matters involving slaves.

If you were white or a free black person accused of a *major* crime — such as murder or horse-stealing — you would have been taken to the Public *Gaol* (the old-fashioned word for jail) in Williamsburg.

Everyone in Williamsburg knew the gloomy Public Gaol on Nicholson Street. The gaol-keeper and his family lived there, too. If you were friends with one of his children, you might have visited and peeked into one of the tiny airless cells where prisoners were kept. You might have caught a

Tom, Tom, the piper's son,
Stole a pig and away he run.
The pig was eat, and Tom was beat,
And Tom went crying down the street.

glimpse of a forger or a murderer chained up awaiting trial. The accused might have a long wait. The General Court met only twice a year.

A person found guilty of a minor crime could get a public flogging at a special whipping post. Sometimes he or she was sentenced to be locked in the stock. The stock had a wooden frame with holes for holding the feet. Stocks were usually set up outside in a public square because part of the punishment was the shame of being seen and insulted by folks who knew you.

People who committed serious crimes, like murder, were sentenced to death. Justice was swift in colonial Williamsburg. Executions took place soon after the verdict.

What happened to slaves who broke the laws?

If an enslaved person was found guilty of killing a master, he or she automatically got the death penalty.

Even attempting to escape from slavery was a serious crime. Slave owners advertised in *The Virginia Gazette*, offering rewards for escaped slaves. If a slave was caught near Williamsburg, he was held in the Public Gaol until his master came to claim him. It was up to the master, not the court, to punish an enslaved person who had run away. Slaves were often punished cruelly by their masters, especially for trying to escape.

In spite of this, many enslaved black people ran away into the woods and swamps outside of town, braving snakes and wild animals rather than having to remain in slavery. Others went into towns such as Fredericksburg and Norfolk, where they tried to blend into the population. Enslaved people often helped hide runaways.

Who made the laws for colonial Williamsburg?

The laws for the colony of Virginia were made by the General Assembly. The General Assembly had two parts — a House of Burgesses and a Council. Both met in Williamsburg in the Capitol building at the head of Duke of Gloucester Street.

The members of the House of Burgesses were *elected*. Virginia's most distinguished citizens — Thomas Jefferson, George Washington, and Patrick Henry, for example — were burgesses. Peyton Randolph, a prominent Williamsburg resident, was Speaker of the House in 1770.

The other body of the General Assembly was the Council. The members of the Council were *appointed* by the king. The English governor was part of the Council. The Council acted as the upper house of the General Assembly. It also advised the governor. The councillors and the governor served as the judges of the General Court.

Why was there an English governor?

Virginia and the other twelve colonies were owned and ruled by England. Because Williamsburg was the capital of Virginia, the English governor's official residence was there. His home and office was the Governor's Palace.

Living in Williamsburg, you would certainly have known the Palace Green in the center of the city. Its great size and elaborate gardens were constant reminders to Williamsburg residents of the power of their "mother country" — Great Britain.

The English governor and the General Assembly worked together in a friendly atmosphere for many years. But by 1770, the friendly feeling was disappearing. You would have begun to hear angry speeches against the British government in Williamsburg streets. In Boston and Philadelphia and other colonial cities, similar voices were being raised.

Why were the colonists angry at the British?

It started with the Stamp Act. In 1765, the British government ordered the colonies to pay taxes on all goods imported from England. It was the first time that Parliament (the British Legislature) had taxed the colonies directly. Before that, the colonial legislatures had controlled taxes on the colonists.

The colonists felt that the British legislature was taking away their rights to be taxed by their own representatives. Like people in the other colonies, Virginians protested strongly. Patrick Henry made a fiery speech against the Stamp Act in the House of Burgesses.

Britain repealed the Stamp Act in 1766, but Parliament kept passing other tax laws for the colonies. The colonies kept protesting. Many Virginians began to refuse to buy certain British goods.

The British dropped some of the taxes, but they kept others. People in the colonies continued to protest. In 1770, news reached Williamsburg that British soldiers had fired on rioters in the colony of Massachusetts. Three years later, they heard that colonists in Boston had staged a protest against a new tax on tea, dumping chests of British tea into the harbor.

Virginians had their own "Tea Party," in the fall of 1774. By this time a movement to break away from British rule was gaining support throughout all thirteen colonies. In 1775, the American Revolution began.

If you had lived in Williamsburg then, you would have been part of it.

Williamsburg today

Today Williamsburg is no longer the capital of Virginia. But part of it looks very much the way it did in the eighteenth century. That's because many of the public buildings, houses, shops, and streets have been restored to look the way they did in colonial times.

The project was started in 1926 by the Reverend W. A. R. Goodwin and John D. Rockefeller, Jr. It was a huge undertaking. Some buildings had to be completely rebuilt. Others were still standing, but were in bad repair. Some houses were moved from one location to another. And some buildings were added to make the picture of colonial life more complete. Colonial Williamsburg opened to the public in 1934. President Franklin D. Roosevelt was at the opening.

Colonial Williamsburg is still an ongoing project. Every year, new exhibits are added or revised. Researchers keep finding new information that shows what it was like . . .

. . . if you lived in Williamsburg in colonial days.

Courtesy of the Colonial Williamsburg Foundation.

To William H. (Bill) Hooks,
who shares my passion for American history

ACKNOWLEDGMENTS
Thanks to all the folks at the Williamsburg Foundation, who shared with me their voluminous records of
colonial life. Especially, I'd like to thank Suzanne Coffman and Donna Sheppard for their help in reading
the manuscript and responding so patiently to my endless questions. I'm particularly grateful to my editor,
Eva Moore, whose expertise and intelligence guided and brought together all the many parts of this project.

ISBN 0-590-92922-4

Book design by Christopher Motil

12 11 10 9   5/0

Printed in the U.S.A.
First Scholastic printing, September 2000